NOTES ON THE HEBREW TEXT
OF JOB I–VI

CHAPTER I

Verse 1. 'A man there was in the land of Uz, Job his name, and that man was perfect and upright, (and) a god-fearer and one who turned aside from evil.'

והיה is curious after the preceding היה. Duhm makes it a colloquialism for ויהי, a frequent opening word of a book, e.g. Joshua, Judges, etc. ICC makes it frequentative (pf. with strong *vav*), which is better. DT 120, DS 83.

וירא copula plus ירא (DG 53 Rem., WL 44, 2*c*), cstr. s. qal ptc. of stative verb. Many read ירא as T, 2 Kenn., MT in i. 8, ii. 3. See WL 60 (f).

וסר might be freq. pf. with strong *vav* after והיה, but better as act. qal ptc. of סור, 'turn aside'; cf. i. 8, ii. 3.

ההוא usual adjectival pronoun for referring to a preceding noun, as against הזה for referring to following noun, GK 136*a*, DS 4.

Verse 2. 'and so there were born to him . . .', thus getting the full force of the strong *vav*, DT 74, DS 76 Rem. 4; cf. 'and it was so' (Genesis i. 7, etc.), this being the direct result of God having spoken. Job's large family and his prosperity are regarded as being the direct outcome of his integrity.

שבעה. Numerals 3–10 without the article precede the plural noun, are in apposition, and differ in gender (so also 3–10 with the article, but in construct). General tendency to use singular as making a group, but the tens have singular only in Ezekiel and P.

Verse 3. 'and his cattle *came to be* . . .' Verb היה does not mean 'to be' so much as 'to come to be'. Hence NT καὶ ἐγένετο.

גמלים. Notice this plural with last radical doubled and preceded by short vowel. This happens mostly, though not exclusively, when last radical is a liquid, DG 141, WL 55. Probable reason is to ensure proper pronunciation of weak consonant.

Note that adjective רב doubles the *beth* in fem. and with all suffixes; root is double-*ayin*.

גדול מכל, 'greater than any of . . .', DG 161 and 48, WL 31.

Verse 4. A whole string of pfs. with strong *vav*, all frequentatives.

אחותיהם. Suffixes irregular, DG 153, WL 185.

Verse 5. הקיפו 3 pl. pf. hiph. of נקף 'make circuit, go round of'. Reference may be to annual feasts (? birthdays); cf. Isaiah xxix. 1 of annual harvest feasts. Translate here as pluperf. Best to take ימי המשתה as object, 'and it used to happen that when they had made the round of feasting-days . . .', then continue the two impfs. with strong *vav* as pluperfs., then resume the frequentatives, 'and he would rise early . . .'

After 'them all' LXX adds: 'and one calf for a sin-offering for their souls', an addition by a scribe who thought that sin-offerings could do more than whole-offerings.

ברכו, either used euphemistically in original or a deliberate alteration, both to avoid the slightest suggestion of cursing God. Note *tsere* because *resh* cannot be doubled. Vowel is lengthened in *ayin-guttural* verbs always with *resh*, mostly with *aleph*, rarely otherwise.

Verse 6. 'Now there came a day when the sons of God came to take their stand by [Moffatt 'present themselves before'; better 'to be in waiting upon'] Jehovah, that Satan also came . . .'

Verse 7. מֵאַיִן, 'from whence' from interrog. adv. אֵי, quite distinct from neg. particle, אַיִן.

The forms שׁוֹט and הִתְהַלֵּךְ are inf. cstr.

Verse 8. הֲשַׂמְתָּ, interrog. (DG 167, WL 28) plus 2 m. s. qal pf. of שׂוֹם or שִׂים, 'to set, place'.

לִבּוֹ. There are two noun forms, לֵב (suffixes as here) and לֵבָב (normal 1st decl. suffixes).

Verse 9. הַחִנָּם. The *he* is the interrog. (DG 167, WL 28).

Verse 10. שַׂכְתָּ from שׂוּךְ I = סוּךְ II, 'to fence', here protectingly as against obstructively as in iii. 23, xxxviii. 8. Some MSS. read סַכֹּתָ, from סכך I, 'to cover', of which the form in iii. 23, xxxviii. 8 could be the hiphil.

מַעֲשֵׂה. Note that the form with *tsere* is cstr.; the absolute has *seghol*.

Verse 11. נַע, 2 m. s. impt. qal of נגע , 'to touch, smite'.

אִם־לֹא, either elliptical '(see) if he do not curse thee', or, better, an oath, 'he will assuredly curse thee'. Oaths with a negative expressed are really positive, e.g. 'I am . . . if I do' means 'I won't', but 'I am . . . if I don't' means 'I will'.

7

Verse 12. בידך. Note tone retracted for the small pause with the accent *zaqeph qaton* (two dots above the line), and the vocal *sheva* becomes a *seghol*. This happens regularly with *athnach* and *silluq*.

Verse 13. שתים, m. pl. act. qal ptc. (שׁתֶה) of שתה, 'to drink'.

יין, S, 1 Kenn. omit; and so in verse 18, where S, LXX, and 2 Kenn. omit. It is not in verse 4. Keep; cf. variation in interrog. in i. 7 and ii. 2.

אחיהם, suffixes irregular, DG 153, WL 185.

Verse 14. בא is pf., and similarly in verses 16, 17, 18.

הבקר is collective, and takes pl. verb. The root means 'to cleave', whence the ox is the animal that cleaves the ground (ploughs) and the בֹּקֶר ('dawn', not 'morning') cleaves the darkness.

חרשׁית. This fem. pl. is strange. Budde suggested it was originally masc., but a copyist altered it under the influence of the next two words.

רעות, fem. pl. qal ptc.; m. sing. is רֹעֶה ; fem. sing. is רֹעָה.

Verse 15. The name of the country (in S.-W. Arabia, usually traders, vi. 19; Ezekiel xxvii. 22 *f*.) is used, and it is feminine, DG 56, WL 56.

ותקחם, 3 f. sing. impf. qal of לקח, 'to take', plus 3 m. pl. suff. plus strong *vav*.

הכו, 3 pl. pf. hiph. of נכה, 'to smite'.

ואמלטה, cohortative with strong *vav*, DT 69, GK 49*e*. More frequent in later books, especially Job; Psalm cxix; Ezra vii. 27–ix. 6 (seventeen times); and Chronicler generally. Here the idea of earnest endeavour may be intended, but generally the co-

hortative is without significance, being used for
first person just as jussive is used with strong *vav* for
second and third persons.

Verse 16. Some would omit אלהים with LXX, but
see 2 Kings i. 12; also Numbers xi. 1; 1 Kings xviii. 38.

Verse 18. עד. The English versions assume that
this is עוד as in the previous verses. So many MSS.,
but MT reading here is possible, though unlikely in
view of verses 16 and 17. Cf. Nehemiah vii. 3; also
1 Samuel xiv. 19; Psalm cxli. 10 (only cases).

Verse 19. באה. Accent on first syllable makes it
3 f. sing. pf.; f. ptc. has accent on last syllable.

ויגע. Strictly this should be fem., but Hebrew is
not strict when subject is remote.

Verse 20. ויקם, 3 m. sing. impf. qal, plus strong
vav, pronounced *way-ya-qom*, with accent on middle
syllable. Similarly *way-ya-goz*, which is from a double-
ayin root.

ארצה, toneless *he-locale*, DG 61, WL 211, of direc-
tion towards.

וישתחו. For this root see DG 145, WL 145, GK
75*kk*.

Verse 21. יצתי, the Qre is the normal form with
aleph written.

ערם is first both times for emphasis.

אמי a double-*ayin* noun, DG 142, WL 190, 191.

מברך, pual ptc., last vowel is normally long, previous vowel is lengthened to compensate for doubled
resh.

Verse 22. זאת. The Hebrew fem. sing. is equivalent
to the Greek neuter plural.

ולא־נתן תפלה, 'nor ascribed unseemliness to God'; cf. Jeremiah xxiii. 13. For idiom, cf. 1 Samuel vi. 5; Joshua vii. 19. This is better than Moffatt's 'nor did he give offence to God'. Ehrlich reads 'prayer', (so Syriac rightly at xxiv. 12), but he translates this 'protest' without justification. In Job vi. 6 the root means 'insipid'. In Targ. Onk. on Deuteronomy i. 1 the verb is used of irreverent talk.

לאלהים, DG 51, WL 44.

CHAPTER II

Verse 2. אי מזה. The interrog. אי (cf. i. 7), when prefixed to other adverbs or pronouns, takes the form אֵי.

Verse 3. ועדנו, copula plus עוד plus 3 m. s. suff., DG 136 (note), WL 110. Followed by ptc. denoting enduring state, DT 135, DS 134 (c) and 135 (f), DG 159, WL 107.

ותסיתני, 2 m. s. impf. hiph. of סות plus 1 s. suff. plus strong *vav*.

Verse 4. נפש. Never translate this word by 'soul', but by 'life, appetite, desire', etc.

לאיש. LXX, S, T omit article correctly, but it is idiomatic in Hebrew, DS 26 (e), GK 126r; cf. 2 Samuel xvii. 17; Joshua ii. 15, etc.

Verse 5. אולם, a very strong adversative. LXX has done well here, and in v. 8, xiii. 3 with οὐ μὴν δὲ ἀλλά.

ויברכך, 3 m. s. impf. pual plus *nun energicum* plus 2 m. s. suff. with tone retracted in pause at end of sentence with *silluq*.

Verse 6. הָנּוּ, rare form. Suffix usually written separately with third person only.

אַךְ, always an adversative, though sometimes slight. Usually (though not here) 'Yes, but', as against אַף (when at it slightest), 'Yes, and'.

Verse 7. וַיַּךְ, 3 m. s. impf. hiph. of נכה plus strong *vav* (apoc.).

Verse 8. LXX adds at end 'without the city', a necessary gloss for non-native readers.

Verse 9. LXX has a long tirade from Job's wife in place of the short question of MT. It is the beginning of that development according to which later Job's wife is, like Eve, regarded as the devil's helper (Augustine, *diaboli adiutrix*). 'How long wilt thou hold out, saying, Behold I will yet wait a little while, expecting the hope of my salvation? For behold thy memorial has disappeared from the earth, sons and daughters, pangs and pains of my womb which I bore in vain with sorrows; and thou thyself sitting down to spend the nights in the open air in the corruption of worms, and I a wanderer and servant from place to place and house to house, waiting for sunset that I may rest from my sorrows and the pangs which now beset me; but say some word against the Lord, and die.'

בָּרֵךְ, 2 m. s. impt. piel.

וּמֻת, 2 m. s. impt. qal; note *qamets* with *vav*, DG 53, WL 44.

Verse 10. כְּדַבֵּר, prep. plus inf. cstr. piel., 'like the speaking of one of the foolish women, thou speakest', though 'thou hast spoken' (reading דִּבַּרְתְּ) would be

better. Duhm retains MT and treats as question,
'Wilt thou speak?' MT could have arisen from
a dittographed *tau*.

גַּם. As this stands it emphasizes the following
אֶת־הַטּוֹב. Merx, Siegfried prefer גַּם אֶת, attaching
it to previous phrase, which is good, though in this
case it is better to omit the אֶת before הָרָע (Duhm,
Gray). An alternative is to keep this, and read
גַּם אֶת אֶת־ (Siegfried, Duhm, Beer).

נְקַבֵּל, Aramaism, elsewhere only in Proverbs xix. 20,
Esther and Chronicles.

שְׂפָתָיו: Note the dual, singular stem with plural
suffixes.

Verse 11. הַבָּאָה, 3 f. s. pf. qal with article used as
relative, so MT, since accent is on penultimate
syllable. Author probably intended the participle
(accent on last syllable), as in LXX.

LXX makes all three friends kings, Eliphaz king of
the Temanites, Baldad (*sic*) tyrant of the Saucheans,
and Zophar king of the Mineans, all of them
Edomite or semi-Edomite tribes.

Verse 12. וַיִּשְׂאוּ, 3 m. pl. impf. qal of נשׂא plus strong
vav, *dagesh* fails with vocal *sheva*.

הִכִּירֻהוּ, 3 pl. pf. hiph. of נכר plus 3 m. s. suff.

הַשָּׁמַיְמָה. LXX omits this, but it is better to retain
both. It is difficult to account for this as gloss, but
MT would be stranger without it.

Verse 13. LXX omits both 'on the ground' and
'and seven nights'. Both may well be glosses.

CHAPTER III

Verse 2. LXX omits 'and Job answered'. It may be due to influence of later introductory formulae.

Verse 3. The tone is retracted thrice to prevent two tone-syllables coming together, producing a better rhythm, GK 29*e*. See also verse 25.

Beer suggested וְלַיִל אִמִּי הָרָת זָכָר 'and the night (in which) my mother conceived a male'. The first and the last changes are unnecessary, but the other two are attractive. הָרָת is 3 f. s. pf. qal of הרה, 'to conceive', a shortened form; cf. Leviticus xxvi. 21. As it stands, MT reads, 'and the night which said (or in which one said) a man-child is conceived'. הֹרָה is 3 m. s. pf. pual, unless it is regarded as passive of qal. LXX has ἰδού, reading הֲרֵה, i.e. Aramaic הֲרֵי for Hebrew הִנֵּה.

Verse 4. יְהִי, 3 m. s. juss. qal of היה, DG 147, WL 145.

תּוֹפַע, 3 f. s. juss. hiph. of יפע, 'shine forth'.

Verse 5. יִגְאָלֻהוּ. LXX, Sym., Theod. all rightly understand the root to be גאל I, 'redeem, get back, claim back', and so RV and (presumably) AVm (challenge it). The essential idea of this root is that it should return to the original owner. Peake, Budde, Gray accept this. The traditional Jewish interpretation is 'defile', גאל II, a late form comparable to געל. This is followed, as often, by AV; so also T, Aq., and probably S, V (obscure).

צַלְמָוֶת. The traditional rendering is 'the shadow of death', as Psalm xxiii. 4; a compound word, so Masoretes and all versions, and, among moderns,

Nöldeke, Budde (now), and Marti. Modern scholars generally read צַלְמוּת, 'deep darkness, so RVm. This is better and is based on parallel words in Arabic and Assyrian.

תִּשְׁכָּן־. Pronounce *tish-kon-*, etc., both vowels short.

כמרירי יום, 'like bitternesses of the day', which means very little, especially since it ought to be the subject. S and T translate this, but retain the subjects of 5*a*. V has 'with bitterness', במרירים. Most moderns read, 'let the blacknesses of the day terrify it', כִּמְרִירֵי; cf. the Syriac כמירא ('blackness' as of a cloud, the night, etc.). So AV and RV, the latter paraphrasing. Cheyne, following LXX, καταραθείη, suggested כְּמוֹ אֹרְרֵי יָם, 'like those that curse the sea', and then deletes as repetition from verse 8.

Verse 6. יִחַדְּ, 3 m. s. juss. qal of חדה, 'rejoice' (*a*-sound because of guttural, WL 144, GK 75*r*); rare in Hebrew, but common in Aramaic. So RV, Driver, Gray, Dillmann, Peake. LXX has εἴη, 'let it not be in the days of the year', reading יְהִי. It is better to follow T, Sym., Saadya (tenth century Babylonian rabbi) and read יֵחַד from יחד, 'let it be joined'; so AV, RVm, Duhm, Budde, Beer. This makes a good parallel.

Verse 8. יקבהו, 3 m. p. juss. qal of קבב II, 'curse' plus 3 m. s. suff.

יום. Schmidt, Cheyne, Gunkel read יָם (sea). This depends upon the interpretation of 'Leviathan' at the end of the verse. If it refers to the sea-monster, as elsewhere in the book, then 'sea' makes an excellent parallel. If the reference is to some monster who eclipses the sun by swallowing it, then MT should stand. This latter idea is common amongst many primitive peoples, but it is not known among the Hebrews. All other moderns retain MT, erroneously we think.

עורר, inf. cstr. poel of עור, 'rouse'. It is usual to prefix *lamedh*, but not essential.

Verse 9. יראה, 3 m. s. imf. qal of ראה (see). We would expect the jussive יֵרֶא (DG 147, WL 144). Normally אל with the *jussive*, and לא with the *imf.* as stronger prohibition, but not properly אל with the imf. (DG 83, WL 85, GK 107*o*).

Verse 10. The negative extends to both clauses, GK 152*z*, DS 175, Rem. 6.

Verse 11. ואבוע. We would expect strong *vav* (i.e. with *qamets*), and similarly in verse 13. Note that the root is בֵּעַ, not an *ayin-vav* verb. It is used eight times in Job, four elsewhere in poetry (post-exilic), and twelve times in P.

Verse 13. ינוח. This impersonal use is not common; cf. verses 17 and 26. Used impersonally in Isaiah xxiii. 12; Nehemiah ix. 28.

Verse 14. הבנים. Article used as relative with ptc.; cf. note on ii. 11.

חרבות למו, '(who build) waste-places for themselves'. So the Versions, and even LXX ('in their swords') which supports the consonants of MT. Delitzsch keeps MT, 'all their massive cities are but desolate ruins at last'. Daiches also retains MT, translating 'fortresses' on basis of the meaning of מחרב in S. Arabian inscriptions. Other suggestions are היכלות

('palaces', Beer in comm.), אַרְמְנוֹת ('fortified palaces',
Olhausen, Dillmann: note pointing, noun is third
decl.), קִרְבוֹת עוֹלָם ('everlasting sepulchres', Cheyne,
Peake), and, best of all, חֲרָמוֹת ('pyramids', after
Arabic *chiram*, Ewald, Budde, Duhm, Gray, Beer (in
Kittel's Bible)).

Verse 15. הַמְמַלְאִים. Article as relative plus m. pl.
piel ptc.; note how *dagesh* fails twice with vocal *sheva*.

Verse 17. רגְזַ. Gray is right in saying this must
mean 'their raging', and not 'their troubling' others.
In either case, Beer's suggestion, following a hint of
Ibn Ezra and Rambam, of רעֲשִׁים is unlikely, since it
does not fit in with the latter half of the sentence.

Verse 18. שָׁאֲנַנּוּ, 3 m. pl. pf. *pa'lel* (cf. IX form in
Arabic of permanent conditions), only form found
in Hebrew. In pause, normal would be שָׁאֲנַנּוּ.

Verse 20. יתֵּן, 3 m. s. imf. qal of נתן . There is no
need to assume on the basis of the versions that they
read a passive. The use in MT is impersonal.

מרי. Notice firm *qamets* since root is double-*ayin*.

Verse 21. הַמְחַכִּים. Article as relative plus m. pl.
ptc. piel of חכה (await).

וַיַחְפְּרֻהוּ, imf. with strong *vav* after a ptc., GK
111*u*, DS 74. There is no need to read וַיַחְפְּשֻׂהוּ
(search), as Beer, nor to change the following *mem*
('more than' which is good) to *kaph* ('like' which is
ordinary) as LXX, S, V, and Beer, Duhm. The
author is a far greater poet than such suggestions
allow.

Verse 22. אֵלִי. An archaic form, such as the original
author loves. Like his use of *Shaddai* ('Almighty'),

16

it is part of the ancient setting of his tale, Exodus
vi. 4 (P).

גִיל, 'exultation' RVm, better than AV and RV,
'exceedingly'. Gratz, Beer and Duhm suggest גַּל
'heap', i.e. grave-heap, on the ground that it secures
a parallelism, but the heaping up of the three words
for 'joy' is better.

כִּי, 'because'. The word strictly does not mean
'when', though often English idiom suggests this.

Verse 23. וַיָּסֶךְ, 3 m. s. imf. hiph. of סוּךְ II (hedge),
though it might be qal (HDB).

Verse 24. לְפָנַי is translatable, as meaning 'before
my every meal', but few scholars are satisfied with it,
even though the Versions support it. Budde and
Peake prefer כְּפִי, 'like my (daily) bread'; Beer לְפִי,
'in proportion to . . .'; Ewald, Hitzig, Dillmann, and
Delitzsch retain MT, but suppose it can mean
'instead of . . .'

וַיִּתְּכוּ, 3 m. pl. imf. qal of נָתַךְ plus strong *vav*,
frequentative after imf., DT 80, GK 111*t*. The verb
is intransitive. Translate 'and have poured forth . . .',
not as in EVV. It is followed by a fem. subject,
DS 157, GK 145*p*.

Verse 25. וַיֶּאֱתָיוּנִי, 3 m. pl. imf. qal of אתה
(Aramaic and late Hebrew 'come') plus 1 s. suff.
plus strong *vav*. Notice survival of original *yod* (cf.
Arabic), as regularly with this verb. The accus. suff.
is found for 'to me' only here with this verb, but for
direct accus. with בוא see xv. 21, xx. 22 plus seven
times in rest of Old Testament, DS 99, Rem. 4.

Verse 26. שָׁלֵוְתִּי. The original *vav* is preserved in
the qal only in this case, DG 143, WL 142, GK 75*bb*.

CHAPTER IV

Verse 2. According to normal syntax, the first line is, 'Has one attempted a word to thee, thou (who) art wearied?' So substantially LXX, 'Hast thou often been spoken to in trouble?' paraphrasing and probably reading דַּבֵּר, inf. cstr. piel, which is better, i.e. 'Has one attempted to speak? . . .' We do not see what is wrong with this, since Job is already out of patience, and Eliphaz is reproving Job for that very thing. Duhm makes a simple question, 'Shall we take up the word to thee, who art disheartened?' The generally accepted rendering is to take the interrogative with the second verb, 'Wilt thou be wearied?' and to make the intermediate words the protasis of a hypothetical sentence with אם understood, GK 150*m*, DT 154. This anomalous construction is seen also in verse 21. So AV, RV, all ancient Versions except LXX, and all moderns except Duhm.

נסה, 3 m. s. pf. piel of נסה 'test', but here 'attempt' (rare, elsewhere only Deuteronomy iv. 34, xxviii. 56, and there with inf. cstr.), Budde, Peake, Gray, RV. An alternative is 1 pl. impf. piel נִסֶּה of the same root, נסה, or 1 pl. impf. qal of נשׂא (cf. Psalm iv. 7), as Duhm. The Versions, except LXX and T (which takes it as a noun, 'Is it because of the testing of the thing? . . .'), have 'begin', either with third person or (Syriac) with first. It is difficult to say whether they read נסה in the sense of 'attempt' or נשׂא, 'lift up'. There are difficulties with both, נשׂא not being found elsewhere with דבר.

18

The pf. is much to be preferred, since two impfs. in a hypothetical sentence is bad.

דבר. It is better to point this as inf. cstr. piel, as Aq., Sym., S, V, LXX, and actually AV and RV.

ותצר. *Chateph* suppressed, *pathach* because of guttural, GK 28*b*.

מלין. Aramaising plural (thirteen times altogether in Job) from מִלָּה. Job has the Hebrew plural in *mem* ten times. GK 87*e*.

יוכל, 3 m. s. impf. qal of יָכֹל 'to be able', DG 129, WL 136.

Verse 3. יסרת, 'instructed, given advice to . . .', unless עָצְרתָ ('thou hast helped') should be read, so many doubtfully.

Verse 4. יקימון, 3 m. pl. impf. of קום with archaic *nun*.

Verse 5. תגע, 3 f. s. impf. qal of נגע, for our neuter.

Verse 6*b*. Transpose the *vav* to before תקותך, so most.

Verse 7. 'Remember now who is he, an innocent one, who perished?'

Verses 10–11. Gray points out the five synonyms for 'lion'. It is said that Arabic has thirty. The first and the last are regular names for 'lion', the others mean 'roarer' (probably), 'young lion', 'strong'.

נתעו. This must be an error for נתצו, 3 m. pl. pf. niph. of נתץ ('shatter'). It cannot be an Aramaism; see ICC, Part II, p. 24.

Verse 12. שמץ, 'whisper', V, Sym., RV; the rendering 'a little' (AV) is due to a late Hebrew meaning of the word; cf. T, S; LXX has a doublet, giving both meanings.

מנהו. Only here, and מנהם only at xi. 20; primitive forms, GK 103*i*, *m*.

Verse 13. תרדמה is not ordinary sleep, but that deep sleep which presages the approach of Deity; cf. Genesis ii. 21, xv. 12. An unusual deep sleep, Proverbs xix. 15.

Verse 14. קראני, 3 m. s. pf. qal of קרא II = קרה ('meet') plus 1 s. suff. The confusion between the two roots is common.

Verse 15. יחלף. The root involves the idea of change, succession; cf. Caliph, the Successor of the Prophet. In Isaiah xl. 31 the meaning is 'change' (as AVm shows), not 'renew', i.e. receive God's strength, not renew their own. Notice רוח is masc. as occasionally viii. 2 and Jeremiah iv. 11 *f*.

תסמר, 3 f. s. impf. piel, סמר, 'bristle up', intensive, not transitive, GK 52*f*. Verb elsewhere only Psalm cxix. 20 in the qal, which some would read here, but this change is not necessary. Nor is it necessary to follow LXX, Beer and Buhl in reading the plural 'hairs', though Gray insists on the plural. Beer (comm.) proposes שְׂעָרָה, and translates 'horror'; so Merx, translating 'whirlwind' as T, both making the piel transitive.

Verse 16. יעמד, 'it stood still', as EVV. LXX, S, Aq. have the 1st person, but that involves the meaning 'rose up', which is incorrect. LXX reads אראה ותמונה לא נגד, and so S, but omitting 'his appearance', but MT is best. V and Douay have a good rendering, 'There stood one, whose countenance I knew not, an image before my eyes', which is legitimate, DS 193, Rem. 4.

Verse 18. תָּהֳלָה. Only here. If correct it means 'error', from an Ethiopic by-form of *tachala* (wander). This is supported by T, עִילָא, but S has תמהא, 'insensibility', perhaps תִּפְלָה, 'unseemliness', as in i. 22. So Hupfeld, Merx, Gratz, etc. These consonants are possibly supported by LXX, σκολιόν (perverseness), perhaps reading some form of the root תפל; so perhaps also V *pravitatem* (depravity, wickedness). The EVV. with 'folly' depend on an impossible derivation from the root הלל in the sense of the Poel (to make a fool of), so Gray. Another suggestion is הַתָּלָה (deception), from the root תלל, Delitzsch, Beer.

Verse 19. יְדַכְּאוּם, 3 m. pl. impf. piel דכא (crush) plus 3 m. pl. suff., 'they (indefinite) crush them'. Some read the pual without suffix, 'they are crushed', but there is no need for this except to provide a closer parallel to the following יְכַתּוּ. Bickell, realizing that this verse is a tristich and seeking to make distichs as the rest, inserts four words and reads, 'He crushes them before the time; he swallows up their glory like the moth', יְדַכְּאֵם לִפְנֵי עֵת וְיַבַלֵּה כְבוֹדָם כְּמוֹ עָשׁ. LXX and T read the singular, making God the subject, and so Bickell.

לִפְנֵי, 'before (the moth)'. This rendering is legitimate, but rare, so that some translate, 'in the manner of', as LXX. Hertz suggested, 'they are crushed from before their Maker', יְדַכְּאוּ מִלִּפְנֵי עֹשָׂם.

יְכַתּוּ, 3 m. pl. impf. hoph. of כתת (beat small),

21

a double-*ayin* form with both consonants strengthened. Usually either the first (Hebrew) or the second (Aramaic) is strengthened, GK 76*g*.

מֵשִׂים, hiph. ptc., but very doubtful formation, since the phrase 'set to heart' has the qal. Merx, Gratz, following LXX, suggest מוֹשִׁיעַ, 'saviour'. MT takes 'for ever' with 'perish', and so V, but T and S take 'for ever' with (?) in the sense of living, dwelling for ever. The text is difficult, and of the various suggestions that of Herz is most attractive, מִבְּלִי שֵׁם 'without name'.

Verse 21. יְתֵרָם, 'their tent-cord', (RV), though this is usually מֵיתָר. Some read יְתֵדָם, 'their tent-peg'. The Versions, except LXX, interpret in the sense of 'remove', and are agreed in the consonants יתרם, T, S and, following them AV and RVm., in the sense of 'their excellency, strength, etc.', and V in the sense of 'their residue'. It is best to retain MT, 'Has not their tent-peg been removed in their midst?' The Versions were all evidently puzzled, Syriac making two attempts, and LXX either reading a completely different text or paraphrasing in desperation, 'for he blows upon them, and they are withered'.

CHAPTER V

Verse 1. עוֹנֶךָ, act. qal ptc. of ענה plus *nun energicum* plus 2 m. s. suff. This is unusual, GK 61*h*, 91*d*. Tone retracted in pause.

Verse 2. לָאֱוִיל. The *lamedh* introduces the accus. as in Aramaic, Syriac and later Hebrew.

Verse 3. וָאָקוֹב, 1 s. impf. qal. קבב (curse) plus strong *vav*, so Aq., T, V and EVV. But וַיֻּקַּב is better ('and was cursed', Cheyne), though if larger change is allowed Cheyne's other suggestion is best, וַיִּרְקַב עֲנָפוֹ פִתְאֹם, 'and his branch suddenly became rotten'. This depends partly upon LXX (was eaten up) and Syriac (and perished). Other suggestions are וְרֵיקָם ('empty', Budde), וַיִּפָּקֵד ('was missed', Budde), and וַיֻּבַּק ('was emptied out', Bevan; cf. Isaiah xxiv. 1, 3).

Verse 4. וִידֻכְּאוּ, 3 m. pl. impf. hithp. plus weak *vav* (copulative).

בַּשַּׁעַר, 'in the gate'. Beer would omit this, but this is where justice was meted out.

Verse 5. אֲשֶׁר קְצִירוֹ, 'whose harvest', but most follow LXX and S, 'that which they have gathered', אֲשֶׁר קָצְרוּ. The last five words of the verse are difficult and corrupt, but no satisfactory solution has been suggested. The Versions vary, and give little help, except that Aq., Sym., S and V all read צְמֵאִים (thirsty) in 5*c*. All suggestions are tentative. For 5*b* either delete as a corrupt dittograph (Duhm. Bickell, Beer), or read וְאֲלֻמָּתָם עָנִי יִקָּחֶה ('and their sheaf the poor taketh', Budde, Gray). For 5*c* either וְשָׁתוּ צְמֵאִים חֵילָם ('the thirsty drink their substance', though Hoffmann, Beer, Gray, etc., object to this on the ground that some drink should be mentioned, e.g. חֲלָבָם, 'their milk') or וְשָׁאַב צָמֵא מִגַּלָּם ('and the thirsty draweth from their well', Duhm, Gray,

Grätz). MT is: 'and to from thorns he taketh it, and a snare gapeth for his wealth'.

Verse 7. יֻלָּד, 3 m. s. pf. pual in pause, with a long *u* anomalously in a closed, sharpened syllable, GK 9*o*. Either the niph. יִוָּלֵד or the hoph. imf. יוּלָד is to be preferred. Our suggestion is that MT found a double tradition, pual and hophal, and preserved both in a mixed form. Most German scholars read יוֹלִד (hiph. 'begetteth trouble'), taking the *lamedh* as indicating the accusative.

בְּנֵי־רֶשֶׁף, 'the sons of Resheph', i.e. flames, Resheph being the ancient Semitic war-god. T thinks of 'demons'; and the other VSS. 'birds', as all at Deuteronomy xxxii. 24, and some elsewhere also.

Verse 11. לָשׂוּם, 'to set up', is difficult, since what follows is no particular consequence of what has gone before. LXX and V read הַשָּׂם, 'who setteth up . . .', which is better.

קֹדְרִים, 'and those that mourn'. Beer suggests קְדֵרִים, 'those that are low', a good parallel; cf. Syriac.

Verse 12. מֵפֵר, ptc. hiph. of פָּרַר (frustrate).

Verse 14. כְּלֵילָה, 'as in the night'. The Hebrew preposition *ke* has a wider significance, being sufficient here, whereas English needs two. GK 118*u*.

Verse 15. The first half of the verse is undoubtedly corrupt; it is meaningless and unbalanced. MT reads, 'But he saveth from the sword from their mouth'. RV follows 20 MSS. (5 Kenn., 15 de R.), S, T and V in reading פִּיהֶם, 'from the sword of their mouth', but, as Gray says, some parallel to 'the poor' is needed in the first half of the verse. Budde suggested מֵחַרְבָּם יָתֹם, '(but he saveth) the father-less from their sword', though he preferred מפיהם יתם, '. . . from their mouth the fatherless'. Gray prefers the former, and Peake the latter. So Siegfried, except that he proposes '. . . from the sword the needy עָנִי'. Any of these last is suitable.

Verse 16. עלתה. The toneless *he* accus. ending survives some fourteen times as a poetic fancy, GK 90*g*, DS 99, Rem. 2. The accus. significance is lost.

Verse 17. הנה. LXX, S, V and 5 MSS., followed by some moderns, chiefly on grounds of metre, omit this. There is no need regularly to insist on exact metrical forms. The absence in 5 MSS. can be accounted for by assimilation in them to the Versions. Both הנה and אשרי can be regarded as genuine, but outside the metrical scheme, e.g. Psalm i. 1.

Verse 18. The הוא ('he') is emphatic, DS 151, DT 160 obs.

יחבש, 3 m. s. impf. qal of חבש (bind) in pause, the normal form being יַחֲבֹשׁ, GK 63*d*.

תרפינה, 3 f. pl. impf. qal of רפא (heal), a *lamedh-he* form by confusion for a *lamedh-aleph* form, DG 125, WL 181, GK 75*qq*.

Verse 20. פדך, 3 m. s. pf. (of certitude, DT 21, DS 61, GK 106*m*) of פדה (redeem) plus 2 m. s. suff. For *lamedh-he* verb with suffixes, DG 229, WL 152 and 265, and especially GK (pages) 530*f*.

Verse 21. בשוט This cannot stand. Read either מִשּׁוֹט, 'from the scourge', as EVV. and almost all moderns, or, if the *beth* is to be kept, בְּשׁוֹט, 'in the scourging (inf. cstr. of verb) of the tongue'. This

25

latter is better, involving no change in the consonantal text, but *beth* and *mem* were very often and easily confused in the older script.

Verse 23. אבני השׂדה. MT may well stand, but Rashi suggested long ago that this might be אַדֹנֵי הַשׂדה (the lords of the countryside), i.e. the elfs, or *jinni* of the 'open country' (שׂדה). This gives point to Hoffmann's suggestion of שֵׁד (demon) for שֹׁד (destruction) in verse 21.

הָשְׁלָמָה, 3 f. s. pf. hoph. of the denominative שׁלם, 'shall be caused to be at peace (with thee)'.

לך. Preposition *lamedh* plus 2 m. s. suff. in pause, thus having the same form as the 2 f. s. suff., DG 51, WL 49.

Verse 24. תחטא, 2 m. s. impf. qal. with the old original meaning 'miss'.

Verse 25. כלח. The word occurs only here and xxx. 2. The Versions guess, but it is evident that the meaning must be 'vigour, strength', the reference being to a hale and hearty old age. Cheyne's suggestion is best: בְּלֵחֲךָ, 'in thy freshness'; cf. Deuteronomy xxxiv. 7.

Verse 27. חקרנוה, 1 pl. pf. qal plus 3 f. s. suff. (for neuter).

שמענה, 2 m. s. imperat. qal plus *nun energicum* plus 3 f. s. suff., but it is better to follow LXX and S and read שְׁמַעְנָהָ, 1 pl. pf. qal with suffix, thus making a true parallel with the first half of the verse.

CHAPTER VI

Verse 2. שָׁקוֹל יִשָּׁקֵל, qal inf. abs. for emphasis, though with 3 m. s. imprf. niphal, but this does happen occasionally, the inf. abs. qal being the simplest form of all, GK 113*w*. Gray points out that LXX read שֹׁקֵל יִשְׁקֹל, ptc. of same stem followed by qal, 'O that the weigher would weigh. . . .', GK 144*e*, which is good.

הַוָּתִי, Qre. 'yawning gulf', and so 'calamity'.

Verse 3. לָעוּ. MT has accent *mil'el* (i.e. on the penultimate syll.), and so it is 3 m. pl. pf. qal of לוֹע (*ayin-vav* verb, 'to swallow up'). It should be לָעוּ with accent *milra'* (i.e. on the last syll.) from לָעָה (*lamedh-he* verb, 'to speak rashly').

Verse 4. עִמָּדִי. Not 'within me', as EVV., but 'with'.

שֹׁתָה, f. s. qal ptc. of *lamedh-he* verb; m. s. has *seghol*.

יַעַרְכוּנִי, 3 m. pl. impf. qal עָרַךְ (array against) plus 1 s. suff. This direct accus. is difficult, but it can stand. The verb is used of 'laying the table' (Psalm xxiii. 5) and of 'ordering the battle line' (Judges xx. 22, etc.), as V here *militant contra me*. LXX (gnaw) suggests יְעָרְקוּנִי, but most moderns prefer יְעַבְּרוּנִי (trouble me excessively, utterly undo).

Verse 5. נָהַק, 'bray' of the ass. Only here and xxx. 7 (of destitute outcasts), but common enough in Arabic and Aramaic.

רִיר חַלָּמוּת. The EVV. 'the white of an egg' is due to the Rabbinic interpretation of the second

27

word as the yolk of an egg, hence 'the saliva [i.e. slime] of the yolk'. LXX has 'in words of dreams', בְּדִבְרֵי חֲלֹמוֹת, so Klostermann, Kamphausen, and (partly) Peake. It is perhaps best to follow RVm, 'the juice of purslain', as most moderns, i.e. the Arabic *chamqa*, which exudes mucilage. The Arabic word means 'fool, idiot', and the plant is so called because it dribbles like an idiot.

Verse 7. המה כדוי לחמי. MT is 'they are like sicknesses of my food', which is clumsy and barely intelligible, even if we knew to what 'they' referred. LXX has βρόμον, but three LXX MSS. read βρῶμον (foul smell), whence we suggest זָהֲמָה כִּדְוַי לַחְמוֹ, 'It (i.e. my soul, appetite, or 'I') finds repulsive as in sickness (cf. v. 14) my food', so Budde, but with בדוי. McNeile proposes זָהֵם חִכִּי לחמי, 'my palate loathes my food', whilst others seek to introduce, on the basis of LXX, the offensive odour of the lion's flesh. Duhm sees in the line a corrupt Aramaic gloss on הלמות in verse 6*b*, reading הֵמוֹ כְּדֵי חֶלְמוֹן, 'that means the yolk of an egg'.

Verse 10. ואסלדה, 1 s. cohort, piel of סלד plus weak *vav*, 'and I would exult (?)'. The word is found only here, and is uncertain. If MT is to remain, then the true meanings 'to be hard (Arabic, צלד)' or 'to draw back (New Hebrew, סלד)' must be forced into some such meaning as 'exult (T)' or 'leap (? for joy)'. It is wiser to emend, and to read either ואעלזה or (better) ואעלסה.

Verse 12. Two simple questions introduced by אם. This is rare, and is due either to a suppressed first part of a double question (GK 150*f*) or to the questions of the previous verse being taken as the equivalent.

Verse 13. הַאִם. The EVV. rightly (according to sense demanded) have 'Is it not . . .', but this cannot be got out of the Hebrew, since אִם in a question thus expects the answer 'No'. It is best to read הִנֵּה, i.e. 'Behold my help (Beer, Budde read עֶזְרָתָה, but this is not necessary) within me is nought'.

Verse 14. 'Loyalty is due from his friend to him that is about to despair and forsake the fear of the Almighty'. חֶסֶד is a covenant word, and means firm and steadfast loyalty to the covenant-bond. מֶס is act. ptc. qal of מסס (dissolve). For *vav* with impf. thus as continuing from the ptc., see Isaiah v. 23, etc., GK 116*x*, DT 137. Peake objects to MT on the ground that it makes Job admit a loss of faith, but we take the ptc. to denote the *fut. instans*, DT 134, this being the reason why the poet did not use the more usual niph. ptc. נָמֵס, which Budde proposes. Others, following S and V, propose לָמָשׁ, 'as for him that withholdeth . . .', but we see no reason to alter MT, though *lamedh* to introduce the substantive is legitimate, GK 143*d*.

Verse 15. כְּאָפִיק נְחָלִים, 'as a channel of *wadies* (that pass away)'. Some would change to כַּאֲפִיקֵי מַיִם (as channels of waters), chiefly to avoid the same word in each half of the verse.

Verse 17. בְּעֵת, cstr. before clause, 'in the time when they wax warm', GK 130*d*, 155*l*; cf. Deuteronomy xxxii. 35 and even Genesis i. 1. Perhaps

29

read שָׁרָב ('parched ground', but properly 'mirage', Isaiah xxxv. 7), Beer, RVm and older scholars, 'shrink', from a Syriac root.

בחמו, *beth* plus inf. cstr. qal of חמם (become warm) plus 3 m. s. suff., but 'it' of the weather is not Hebrew. Budde, Beer suggest בְּחֹם זְ, 'when it is hot, then (GK 143*d*, DS 106) they are consumed . . .'.

Verse 18. 'The paths of their way twist about', so AV, RVm, and Delitzsch, Davidson, Hitzig and Budde, referring to the *wadies*, but most moderns and RV read אָרְחוֹת יְלַפְּחוּ, 'the caravans divert their way', which is much better, in view of succeeding verses.

Verse 19. Read אָרְחוֹת, 'caravans', as EVV.

Verse 20. Read בָּטְחוּ and עֲדֵיהֶם.

Verse 21. MT is 'For now ye are become it'; cf. BDB, p. 226, II*e*, or, taking the Kethib, it is said by some to mean, 'For now ye are become nothing', as AV, RV, but this rendering is impossible, and demands the Hebrew לְאַיִן. It is best to read, 'So (כֵּן, Houbigant and J. D. Michaelis) are ye become to me (לִי, LXX, S)', as most moderns.

Verse 22. הבו. The root יהב is the common Aramaic root for 'give', found only in qal impert. in Hebrew with *yod* missing.

Verse 25. נמרצו. The root occurs thrice only apart from here: xvi. 3; 1 Kings ii. 8; Micah ii. 10. The 'forcible' of EVV. is from Ibn Ezra and Qimchi, but it is a conjecture. If MT is to stand, the root must mean either 'to press with the fingers' or 'to be sick', or again, by metathesis, 'to be sour, acid'. The meaning of the niph. form might be 'pressed', 'made sick', or 'irritated' (not 'irritating', which would be qal). It is best to follow T and Rashi, and translate 'sweet', reading נמלצו as many moderns.

Verse 26. ולרוה. MT is translatable but וּלְרִיב, 'and to contend', so McNeile, Beer (in Kittel). This obtains a good parallel.

נאש or נואש, niph. ptc. of יאש (despair).

Verse 27. תפלו. It is better to translate as RV, 'ye would cast lots upon the fatherless'. There is no need to assume the qal תִּפְּלוּ as AV, 'ye would fall upon . . .', nor to read עֲלֵי תָם (upon the perfect), as Bickell, Gratz and Duhm.

תכרו, 'and ye would make a bargain of . . .', parsing as 2 m. pl. impf. qal of כרה II (buy), and so RV. Some would read תָּכֹרוּ ('turn round upon', from כרר). AV 'dig (a pit)' is from כרה I.

Verse 28. אם, of an oath, i.e. 'I swear I will not lie'.

Verse 29. צדקי בה, lit. 'my righteousness is in it', as AV, RVm; whilst RV paraphrases.

Printed in Great Britain by
The Camelot Press Ltd., London and Southampton